The Only Academic Phrasebook You'll Ever Need

600 Examples of Academic Language

LUIZ OTÁVIO BARROS

Copyright © 2016 Luiz Otávio Barros

All rights reserved. No part of this book may be reproduced, stored in a retrieval system, or transmitted in any form, or by any means, electronic, mechanical, photocopying, recording or otherwise, without prior permission of the author.

ISBN: 1539527751
ISBN-13: 978-1539527756

By the same author:

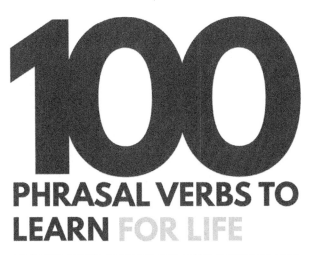

100 PHRASAL VERBS TO LEARN FOR LIFE

VOCABULARY EXPANSION FOR HIGH-INTERMEDIATE AND ADVANCED STUDENTS

LUIZ OTÁVIO BARROS

CONTENTS

	Acknowledgements	vii
	This Book in a Nutshell	ix
1	Establishing a Research Territory	1
	Grammar and Vocabulary Tips 1	4
	Quiz 1	6
2	Describing Research Gaps	7
	Grammar and Vocabulary Tips 2	10
	Quiz 2	13
3	Stating Your Aims	14
	Grammar and Vocabulary Tips 3	17
	Quiz 3	21
4	Describing the Scope and Organization of Your Paper	22
	Grammar and Vocabulary Tips 4	25
	Quiz 4	29
5	General Literature Review	30
	Grammar and Vocabulary Tips 5	33
	Quiz 5	35
6	Referencing	36
	Grammar and Vocabulary Tips 6	39
	Quiz 6	42
7	Sampling and Data Collection	43
	Grammar and Vocabulary Tips 7	48
	Quiz 7	52
8	Data Analysis and Discussion	53
	Grammar and Vocabulary Tips 8	60
	Quiz 8	64
	Quiz Answers	65
	How This Book Came into Being	69

ACKNOWLEDGMENTS

Special thanks to Dr. Patricia Friedrich, from Arizona State University, for her feedback on the final manuscript.

LUIZ OTÁVIO BARROS

THIS BOOK IN A NUTSHELL

Q: *I know what I want to say, but I can't find the right words - or the right tone. Will a phrasebook like this be useful?*
A: Yes. It will enable you to express yourself with more precision and clarity. For example, you will learn how to write "This study addresses the issue of […]" rather than "This study talks about […]." Or "While there is wide agreement that […]" instead of "Although a lot of people agree that […]." Think of this book as a short, no-nonsense databank of sentence frames to help you write essays, term papers, reports, dissertations and theses, using the right words and the right style.

Q: *Great! I don't even know what an academic paper looks like!*
A: Please keep in mind that *The Only Academic Phrasebook You'll Ever Need* does NOT cover the basics of academic writing. It will NOT teach you how to write thesis statements, develop and refine your arguments or create coherent paragraphs, just to name a few key academic writing skills. *The Only Academic Phrasebook You'll Ever Need* is, as the title suggests, essentially a phrasebook. It is NOT a comprehensive textbook or research guide.

Q: *English is not my first language. Can I use this book?*
A: It depends on your level of proficiency. Ideally, you should be an upper-intermediate or advanced student to make the most of it.

Q: *I'm a native speaker of English, but I keep getting things like "there/their/they're" or "affect/effect" wrong. Will this book help me?*
A: Yes. As well as 600 sentence "templates", you will find 80 grammar, vocabulary and punctuation tips, written with both native and non-native speakers in mind.

I hope you enjoy using this book as much I enjoyed writing it.

CHAPTER 1
ESTABLISHING A RESEARCH TERRITORY

Establishing a research territory (Swales and Feak, 2009) means setting a context for your research. This usually includes a brief literature review as well as reference to other key developments in your research area. Your goal should be to establish yourself as a legitimate member of that particular research community. Sentences 1-50 will help you do that.

1. _____ has received a lot of research attention.
2. _____ has led to a renewed interest in _____.
3. In recent years, researchers have become increasingly interested in

4. The last few years have seen an increased interest in _____.
5. Numerous studies have investigated _____.
6. An increased interest in _____ **has emerged**[1] in recent years.

The words and phrases in bold are further explored at the end of each chapter.

7. _____ has been extensively researched.
8. _____ has been field-tested by _____.
9. _____ has been widely studied **due to**[2] _____.

On the use of active/passive voice (1):
Sentences 1-6 are in the active voice (i.e., the subject of the sentence performs the action of the sentence), while sentences 7-9 are in the passive voice (i.e., the subject of the sentence receives the action).
Some scholars frown upon the use of passive voice, especially when the agent (i.e., "the doer") of the action is not completely obvious. The decision of whether to use active (e.g.: "We interviewed forty students.") or passive voice (e.g.: "Forty students were interviewed.") has to be made in context, depending on the research discipline. Be sure to follow the guidelines set by your instructors.

A number of recent studies have...
10. examined _____.
11. investigated _____.
12. focused on _____.
13. reported on _____.
14. reported that _____.
15. linked _____ to _____.
16. addressed the issue of _____.
17. shown that _____.
18. suggested that _____.
19. found concrete evidence that _____.
20. directly compared _____ and _____.
21. looked into the effects of _____ on _____.

Over the years, an enormous amount of research has been...
22. done on _____.
23. carried out in an attempt to _____.
24. conducted to determine _____.
25. **devoted to**[3] _____.

Recent studies have explored the...
26. use of _____ as _____.
27. impact of _____ on _____.
28. differences/similarities between _____ and _____.
29. **role** of _____ **in/as** _____.[4]

The role of _____ has been...
30. extensively studied in recent years.
31. grossly misunderstood.
32. largely overlooked.
33. overshadowed by _____.
34. viewed as _____.

Considerable research attention has been...
35. paid to ____.
36. devoted to ____.
37. directed toward ____.

38. **It is**[5] now generally accepted that ____.
39. ____ has generated a wealth of data on ____.
40. **Within**[6] this area of investigation, a number of studies ____.

Ample **evidence**[7] exists...
41. regarding ____.
42. to support ____.
43. to prove (that) ____.
44. to suggest (that) ____.
45. to support the view that ____.
46. to support the hypothesis that ____.
47. to suggest a connection between ____ and ____.

48. The study of ____ has become a key aspect of ____.
49. ____ is an emerging research area in the field of ____.
50. In 1799, Smith and Jones collaborated to investigate ____.

Throughout this book:
1799 = Insert the year.
[N] = Insert a number.
Smith/Jones = Insert the scholar's name.

Reference:
Feak, C. B., & Swales, J. M. (2009). *Telling a research story: Writing a literature review.* Ann Arbor, MI: University of Michigan Press.

GRAMMAR AND VOCABULARY TIPS 1

1. Tense usage: **have/has + past participle**

Original sentence: *An increased interest in _____ has emerged in recent years.*

Has emerged is an example of the so-called present perfect tense. Use the present perfect rather than the simple past (*emerged*) with time expressions such as *recent, recently* and *in the past/last* [N] *years*:

WRONG: "A number of studies were conducted in the past ten years."
RIGHT: *A number of studies have been conducted in the past ten years.*

2. Linking ideas: **due to**

Original sentence: *_____ has been widely studied due to _____.*

Due to is a more formal way of saying *because of*. It is followed by a noun phrase, not a clause:

a. *...because it was discovered that.../...due to the discovery that...*
(NOT "...due to it was discovered that...")
b. *...because there are a lot of relevant studies.../...due to the number of relevant studies.*
(NOT "...due to there are a lot of...")

3. Tricky phrase: **devoted to**

Original sentence: *Over the years, an enormous amount of research has been devoted to _____.*

If you use a verb after *devoted to*, it must be in the *-ing* form:

The first part of the questionnaire was devoted to investigating (NOT "devoted to investigate") *the subjects' exercise habits.*

The *-ing* form must be used because *to* in this case is a preposition (as in *get used to living, look forward to hearing*), not part of the infinitive.

4. Tricky pair: **role in/role as**

Original sentence: *Recent studies have explored the role of _____ in/as _____.*

Compare the use of *in/as* after *role*:

This study examines...
a. *The role of obesity as a risk factor.*
b. *The role of memory in language acquisition.*
c. *The role of meditation in treating cancer.*

5. Style: **contracted forms**

Original sentence: *It is now generally accepted that _____.*

Avoid contracted forms in academic writing.

USE: *It is…/There has…/I did not…/We do not…*
AVOID: *It's…/There's…/I didn't…/We don't…*

6. Key word: **within**

Original sentence: *Within this area of investigation, a number of studies _____.*

Here are a few common uses of *within*: within [N] days, the space of [N] years, the scope of this paper, the limitations of this study, the [academic] community.

7. Count vs. non-count: **evidence**

Original sentence: *Ample evidence exists (regarding) _____.*

Like *information, advice* and *equipment, evidence* is uncountable:

WRONG: "~~Many evidences~~ support Smith's hypotheses."
RIGHT: *A lot of/Ample/Overwhelming evidence supports Smith's hypotheses.*

Now take the quiz on the next page to check your progress. The quiz is based on points 1-7 on pages 4 and 5.

QUIZ 1

Correct the mistakes, if any, in sentences 1-6. Answers on page 65.

1. In the past few years, there was a great deal of controversy surrounding soy foods, mostly due to recent research.

2. The last four decades have seen incredible human progress across South America.

3. Since the 1990s, there has been a dramatic increase in the number of people with Alzheimer's.

4. Recent studies have risen a number of key questions regarding the impact of CCTV on crime.

5. In 2014, an important study by Smith et al. rose a number of concerns about online data collection.

6. It is not within the scope of this paper to propose solutions to this issue. This study is simply devoted to understand the problem.

CHAPTER 2
DESCRIBING RESEARCH GAPS

After you have defined your general research territory, the next step is to identify a research gap worth exploring. In other words, you should explain to your audience what kinds of problems/questions remain controversial or unresolved in your field of study so that you can create a unique research niche. Sentences 51-94 will help you do that.

51. _____ deserve(s) more research attention.
52. Most _____ studies have focused mainly on _____.
53. The vast majority of the work in this area has focused on _____.
54. **There**[8] is limited research investigating _____.
55. There is scant evidence that _____.
56. **To date**[9], no study has looked specifically at _____.
57. To the best of my/our knowledge, no study has focused on _____.
58. Few studies have investigated the impact of _____.
59. **Little**[10] research has been done on _____.
60. Little is known about _____.
61. Relatively little is understood about _____.
62. To date, scant attention has been paid to _____.
63. Since _____, little has been written about _____.
64. Few attempts have been made to investigate the role of _____.

On the use of active/passive voice (2):
Notice how sentences 59-64, which are in the passive voice, shift the focus away from the agent (i.e., "the doer") toward the action. As a rule, in the humanities and social sciences, the fact that there is an agent often needs to be acknowledged, while in the natural sciences preference tends to be given to omitting the agent. Be sure to follow the guidelines set by your institution.

Previous research has largely **overlooked**[11] the...
65. role of _____.
66. importance of _____.
67. significance of _____.
68. issue of _____.
69. challenges associated with _____.
70. ways in which _____.
71. possibility that _____.

72. Previous studies have disregarded _____.
73. Research on _____ has relied primarily on _____.
74. Previous research in the field of _____ has been restricted to _____.
75. A limited number of studies have addressed _____.
76. Existing research has focused on _____ but failed to explore _____.
77. Within the field of _____, a number of crucial questions remain unanswered.
78. Few studies in the field of _____ have **sought**[12] to examine _____.
79. Remarkably few studies have been designed to _____.
80. The evidence points to _____. **However**[13], the role of _____ is still poorly understood.
81. _____ is an important area of enquiry; however, relatively little is known about _____.
82. Most scholars seem to agree that _____. However, there continues to be debate about _____.
83. _____ has been the subject of research since _____. However, _____.
84. **A number of**[14] studies have shown that _____. However, important questions regarding _____ remain unanswered.
85. Available data regarding _____ are contradictory.
86. Smith's research is **not without**[15] controversy.
87. Smith's study has been subject to a great deal of criticism.
88. Smith's attempts to establish a link between _____ and _____ are questionable.

89. Critics of _____ argue that _____.
90. The limitations of _____ are increasingly apparent.
91. **There**[16] remain many unanswered questions about _____.
92. While there has been a great deal of research on _____, very few studies _____.
93. Although a considerable body of research has _____, less attention has been paid to _____.
94. **Despite**[17] decades of research on _____, _____ has been less than satisfactory.

GRAMMAR AND VOCABULARY TIPS 2

8. Tricky trio: **there/they're/their**

Original sentence: *There is limited research investigating _____.*

There (not here/indicates existence), *they're* (they are) and *their* (possessive adjective) are different words. Here's a sentence to help you remember the difference:

There are a lot of reasons why they're expecting their grades to improve.

9. Style: **to date**

Original sentence: *To date, no study has looked specifically at _____.*

To date is a slightly more formal way of saying *until now/so far*.

10. Count vs. non-count: **few/little**

Original sentence: *Little research has been done on _____.*

Notice the use of *little* with *research* (uncountable) and *few* with *studies* (countable). Here are some other examples:

a. *Little information/few details*
b. *Little advice/few suggestions*
c. *Little time/few minutes*

11. Tricky pair: **overlook/oversee**

Original sentence: *Previous research has largely overlooked the (role of) _____.*

Don't confuse *overlook* (fail to notice) with *oversee* (supervise):

a. *It is believed that the accident happened because a number of safety checks were overlooked.*
b. *The project was overseen by the local team.*

12. Key word: **seek**

Original sentence: *Few studies in the field of _____ have sought to examine _____.*

Sought is the past and past participle of *seek*, which is a more formal way of saying *try to do or obtain something*. For example: *seek funding for a project, employment, medical advice, new ways of doing something, to protect the democratic rights of citizens.*

13. Punctuation: **however**

Original sentence: *The evidence points to _____. However, the role of _____ is still poorly understood.*

Notice the use of periods, commas and semi-colons with *however* to signal that a counterpoint will follow:

a. *I thought the figures were correct. However, I have discovered some errors.*
b. *I thought the figures were correct; however, I have discovered some errors.*
c. *I thought the figures were correct. I have, however, discovered some errors.*

Don't use a comma before *however* if it's followed by an independent clause:

"I thought the figures were ~~correct, however, I have~~ discovered some errors."

14. Tricky pair: **a number of/the number of**

Original sentence: *A number of studies have shown that _____.*

Notice the use of a plural verb after *a number of* (a lot of) and a singular verb after *the number of*:

a. *A number of scholars are exploring this possibility.*
b. *The number of deaths is currently unknown.*
c. *A number of research papers have demonstrated that the number of divorces has dropped.*

15. Tricky phrase: **not without**

Original sentence: *Smith's research is not without controversy.*

Not without is a double negative that means *with*:

a. *Not without reason, some scholars are skeptical of the entire notion of causation.* (They have their reasons.)
b. *The study is not without flaws.* (It has its flaws.)

16. Subject/verb agreement: **there**

Original sentence: *There remain many unanswered questions about _____.*

Notice the use of a singular/plural verb after *there*. To decide which form to use, try replacing the verb with *is* and *are*. *Is* = singular and *are* = plural:

a. *There seems to be a problem.* (There is a problem.)
b. *There seem to be a number of problems.* (There are a lot of problems.)

17. Linking ideas: **despite**

Original sentence: *Despite decades of research on _____, _____ has been less than satisfactory.*

Despite must be followed by a noun phrase or an *-ing* verb rather than a clause:

a. *...although the results were negative.../...despite the negative results...*
(NOT "...~~despite the results were~~ negative...")
b. *...although the findings are inconclusive, they suggest.../...despite being inconclusive, the findings suggest...*
(NOT "~~despite they are~~ inconclusive...")

In spite of means the same as *despite* and is used in a similar way.

Now take the quiz on the next page to check your progress.

QUIZ 2

Correct the mistakes, if any, in sentences 1-6. Answers on page 65.

1. To the best of my knowledge, there are relatively few researches in this area.

2. The evidence supporting a low-carb diet are moderate at best.

3. The number of studies investigating the use of educational technology has dropped.

4. In recent years, a number of scholars have addressed this issue.

5. A number of longitudinal studies have examined this question; however, not all of them are replicable in other contexts.

6. Despite claims to the contrary, there seem to be ample evidence that this is the case.

CHAPTER 3
STATING YOUR AIMS

After you have established your research territory and identified a relevant gap in the literature, you should show your reader how exactly your study intends to bridge this gap. Sentences 95-160 will help you do that.

This study was…
95. commissioned by _____.
96. carried out to examine _____.
97. conducted in order to investigate _____.
98. **undertaken**[18] to determine _____.

Use study, paper, article, essay, report *or* literature review *as appropriate.*

This study…
99. is concerned with _____.
100. is aimed at _____.
101. provides an overview of _____.
102. looks at how _____.
103. critically reviews _____.
104. **addresses**[19] the issue of _____.
105. examines the relationship between _____ and _____.
106. attempts to establish the connection between _____ and _____.
107. discusses ways **in which**[20] _____.
108. provides data that will _____.
109. provides detailed information on _____.
110. offers an analysis of _____.
111. discusses the role of _____ in _____.
112. considers the role of _____ as _____.
113. **explores**[21] the link between _____ and _____.

This study sought to…
114. **assess**[22] _____.
115. describe _____.
116. test _____.
117. shed light on _____.
118. provide detailed information on _____.

The aim of this study is/was to…
119. address the **issue**[23] of _____.
120. determine the effect of _____.
121. evaluate the effectiveness of _____.
122. identify the characteristics of _____.
123. extend this area of investigation by _____.
124. assess the impact of _____ on _____.
125. provide a detailed account of _____.
126. clarify the role of _____.
127. investigate whether _____.
128. discuss the **extent to**[24] which _____.
129. test the feasibility of _____.
130. examine the variables associated with _____.
131. understand the nature of _____.
132. collect and **analyze**[25] data on _____.

133. The notion of _____ underlying this study is a broad one.
134. One of the central claims of this study is that _____.
135. The aim of this study is **twofold**[26]. The first is to _____. The second is to _____.
136. The theoretical framework underpinning this study is/was _____.

In this study, I/we…
137. report on _____.
138. set out to investigate _____.
139. seek to determine (whether) _____.
140. examine the degree to which _____.

141. consider the extent to which _____.
142. discuss the implications of _____.
143. investigate the association between _____ and _____.
144. establish the main factors behind _____.
145. **attempt**[27] to shed some light on _____.

On the use of I/my/we/our:
Sciences: In order to sound objective and impersonal, scientific writers tend to avoid the use of the first person. However, conventions are changing, and in some cases the first person is becoming more widely accepted, so be sure to ask your instructor first.
Humanities: Scholars in these fields tend to value assertiveness and agency (i.e., who does what), so the first person is often - though not always -appropriate. Make sure you follow your department's conventions.

In the present study, I/we...
146. describe a framework for _____.
147. propose a series of solutions for _____.
148. provide a theoretical basis for _____.
149. undertake an analysis of _____.
150. highlight the key differences between _____ and _____.

My/Our main goal is/was to...
151. gain a better understanding of _____.
152. gain insight into _____.
153. determine **if/whether**[28] _____.
154. explore the range of factors that influence _____.
155. further my/our understanding of _____.
156. gather **information**[29] about _____.
157. investigate the effect of _____ on _____.
158. determine the importance of _____.
159. identify the key variables affecting _____.
160. understand the mechanisms **underlying**[30] _____.

GRAMMAR AND VOCABULARY TIPS 3

18. Key words: **carry out/conduct/undertake**

Original sentence: *This study was undertaken to determine _____.*

When *carry out, conduct* and *undertake* mean *do*, they are often used with these words: *a survey, an investigation, an inquiry, a test, a study, research (NOT "a research"), an analysis.*

Carry out is slightly less formal than *conduct* and *undertake*.

19. Key word: **address**

Original sentence: *This study addresses the issue of _____.*

The verb *address* (deal with) is very common in academic writing. It is often used with these words: *an issue, a problem, (someone's) concerns, (someone's) needs.*

20. Relative clauses: **in which**

Original sentence: *This study discusses ways in which _____.*

Notice how the use of *in which* helps to make a sentence more formal:

a. *This is the place where the study was carried out. (neutral)*
b. *These are the premises in which the study was conducted. (more formal)*

21. Tricky pair: **explore/exploit**

Original sentence: *This study explores the link between _____ and _____.*

Remember: *Explore* (examine, investigate) is not the same as *exploit* (take unfair advantage of).

22. Tricky pair: **assess/access**

Original sentence: *This study sought to assess _____.*

Don't confuse *assess* (evaluate) with *access* (e.g.: access the internet).

23. Key phrase: **the issue of**

Original sentence: *The aim of this study is/was to address the issue of _____.*

The issue of can be followed by:

a. A noun: *The issue of homelessness.*
b. A *wh-* word: *The issue of why Chinese is so difficult to learn./The issue of when a fetus can be considered a person.*
c. *Whether or not to*: *The issue of whether or not to pass the bill.*
d. *Whether or not* + clause: *The issue of whether astrology can be considered a science.*

24. Key word: **extent**

Original sentence: *The aim of this study is/was to discuss the extent to which _____.*

Use *to+ extent* to show how far something is true:

a. *To a certain extent, what Smith et al. argue is relevant.* (But some of their arguments may be less relevant.)
b. *To what extent is this true?* (This may well be true, but perhaps not entirely.)
c. *Economic and social factors are, to a large extent, responsible for the current state of affairs.* (They are mostly, but not entirely, to blame.)

25. Spelling: **s/z**

Original sentence: *The aim of this study is/was to collect and analyze data on _____.*

Analyze is spelled with a z in American English and with an s in British English. Other verbs that follow the same pattern include *organize, memorize* and *realize*.

26. Affixation: -fold

Original sentence: *The aim of this study is twofold. The first is to _____. The second is to _____.*

You can use words such as *twofold, fivefold, tenfold* as adjectives or adverbs:

a. *There was a twofold increase in the number of casualties.* (adjective with the noun *increase*)
b. *The number of casualties increased twofold.* (adverb with the verb *increase*)

Don't use *by* before number + *fold*:
WRONG: "Profits increased by threefold."

27. Style: attempt

Original sentence: *In this study, I/we attempt to shed some light on _____.*

Attempt is a more formal way of saying *try*. It can be both a noun (e.g.: *my attempts to…*) and a verb (e.g.: *I will attempt to…*).

28. Tricky pair: if/whether

Original sentence: *My/Our main goal is/was to determine if/whether _____.*

You can use both *if* and *whether* to express alternatives:

We will try to determine if/whether the initial hypothesis is valid.

Whether is preferable in formal writing. Use *whether*, NOT *if*:

a. Directly before *or not*: *It is important to determine whether or not the initial hypothesis was valid.*
b. After prepositions (*in, about, for, to* etc.): *There is some disagreement about whether or not the dataset is reliable.*

29. Count vs. non-count: information

Original sentence: *My/Our main goal is/was to gather information about _____.*

Remember: *Information* is an uncountable noun. It is WRONG to say "two informations", "many informations" or "an information."

30. Key word: **underlying**

Original sentence: *My/Our main goal is/was to understand the mechanisms underlying ____.*

Other common phrases with *underlying* (fundamental) include: *the underlying cause of..., premise of..., assumption behind..., reason for...*

Now take the quiz on the next page to check your progress.

QUIZ 3

Correct the mistakes, if any, in sentences 1-6. Answers on page 66.

1. The informations in chart 1 were collected in August 2015.

2. This study will try to determine if or not the initial hypotheses were valid.

3. At this point it is hard to access the extent to which these findings will have a sizeable impact on language teaching.

4. Although there seem to be evidence that this is the case, the underlying mechanisms remain unclear.

5. This paper addresses the issue of urban violence and exploits ways in which we can make our cities safer.

6. This study was undertaken as an attempt to assess the effects of meditation on blood pressure.

CHAPTER 4
DESCRIBING THE SCOPE AND ORGANIZATION OF YOUR PAPER

To make your research paper as reader-friendly as possible, you should be clear about how much ground you intend to cover and how you will organize your ideas logically. Sentences 161-216 will help you do that.

This paper provides an overview of…
161. findings from recent _____.
162. recent developments in _____.
163. issues relating to _____.
164. the current debates about _____.
165. the main types of _____.
166. the **effect**[31] of _____ on _____.
167. the critical factors influencing _____.
168. the basic concepts of _____.
169. the available official data on _____.
170. **current**[32] research on _____.
171. _____ theory and **its**[33] ramifications.

Use study, paper, article, essay, report *or* literature review *as appropriate.*

This paper…
172. is divided into [N] sections.
173. is divided into [N] broad parts.
174. is organized into [N] distinct sections.
175. consists of [N] parts.
176. is comprised of [N] sections.
177. **comprises**[34] [N] parts.

Section [N] provides...
178. an overview of ____.
179. a reasonably comprehensive overview of ____.
180. a brief introduction to ____.
181. a theoretical introduction to ____.
182. a basic theoretical **framework**[35] for ____.
183. **broad**[36] guidance on ____.
184. general guidelines on ____.
185. background information on ____.
186. the foundation for ____.
187. a concise analysis of ____.
188. important contextual information **regarding**[37] ____.

Use section, part *or* chapter *as appropriate.*

Part [N]...
189. deals with ____.
190. is dedicated to ____.
191. details the findings of ____.
192. addresses the issue of ____.
193. considers the nature of ____.
194. outlines some of the **key**[38] principles behind ____.

In section [N], I/we...
195. review the existing literature on ____.
196. provide arguments supporting ____.
197. present some fundamental ideas underlying ____.
198. identify the key factors behind ____.
199. present a theoretical framework for ____.
200. **discuss**[39] the main reasons for ____.

In chapter [N],…
201. the concept of _____ is further explored.
202. _____ is/are quantitatively assessed.
203. a qualitative analysis of _____ is carried out.
204. the data are analyzed quantitatively/qualitatively.

On the use of active/passive voice (3):
Sentences 201-204 are in the passive voice. Remember to follow your department's guidelines on the use of active/passive voice.

This paper is organized into [N] main…
205. parts, the first of which deals with _____.
206. sections. Section [N] examines _____. Section [N] looks at _____.
207. parts, **both of which**[40] focus on _____.

208. The **remainder**[41] of this paper is structured/organized as follows. Section [N] _____. The next section then _____.

This paper is not intended to be a comprehensive…
209. analysis of _____.
210. evaluation of _____.
211. overview of _____.
212. review of _____.
213. survey of _____.

214. An extended discussion of _____ is beyond the scope of this paper.
215. An **in-depth**[42] analysis of _____ is not within the scope of this article.
216. _____ lies outside the scope of the present study.

GRAMMAR AND VOCABULARY TIPS 4

31. Tricky pair: **affect/effect**

Original sentence: *This paper provides an overview of the effect of _____ on _____.*

When you talk about influence, *effect* is a noun, and *affect* is a verb:

a. *Differences in social status may affect participants' answers, which will have a significant effect on the results.*
b. *The effects of the diet affected participants in different ways.*

Effect as a verb means to cause something to happen. (e.g.: *effect a peace settlement, effect lasting change*)

32. Tricky pair: **actual/current**

Original sentence: *This paper provides an overview of current research _____ on _____.*

Remember: *Actual* (real), which means *present* in many languages, cannot replace *current*.

33. Tricky pair: **its/it's**

Original sentence: *This paper provides an overview of _____ theory and its ramifications.*

Don't confuse *its* (possessive adjective) with *it's* (it is):

It's an interesting study, and its aim is to discuss the main tenets of Smith's theory.

34. Tricky pair: **consist/comprise**

Original sentence: *This paper comprises [N] parts.*

Both *consist* and *comprise* are used to describe what something is 'made of.' *Comprise* is more formal than *consist* and doesn't take *of* in the active voice:

Section one consists of/ comprises (NOT "~~comprises of~~") *ten multiple choice questions.*

Comprised of is possible in the passive voice:

This paper is comprised of five sections.

35. Key word: **framework**

Original sentence: *Section [N] provides a basic theoretical framework for _____.*

The word *framework* (basic structure) is very common in academic writing. It can be used in a number of ways:

a. *This study is flawed and lacks a conceptual framework.*
b. *The agreement provides a legal framework for reciprocity.*
c. *The author provides no theoretical framework for her study.*
d. *The framework for this analysis was structured around existing research.*

36. Key word: **broad**

Original sentence: *Section [N] provides broad guidance on _____.*

Other words you can use with *broad* include *range of..., array of..., scope of..., overview of...*

37. Linking ideas: **regarding**

Original sentence: *Section [N] provides important contextual information regarding _____.*

Besides *regarding*, you can use *with regard to* or *in regard to*. *As regards* is slightly less formal. "In regards to" and "with regards to" are considered non-standard.

38. Key word: **key**

Original sentence: *Part [N] outlines some of the key principles behind _____.*

You can use *key* (very important) to describe a number of things: *a key issue, factor, point, role, word, concept.*

39. Tricky word: **discuss**

Original sentence: *In section [N], I/we discuss the main reasons for _____.*

Discuss is NOT followed by the preposition *about*:

In section two, we discuss (NOT "~~discuss about~~") *the most relevant findings.*

40. Tricky pair: **both of which/all of which**

Original sentence: *This paper is organized into [N] main parts, both of which focus on _____.*

Both of which refers to two things, while *all of which* refers to three or more things:

a. *The other studies, both of which were conducted in the USA, produced similar results.*
b. *This paper comprises three parts, all of which are interconnected.*

Notice the punctuation:

a. CORRECT: *Two studies were reported, both of which were controlled trials.*
b. WRONG: *Two studies were ~~reported. Both of which~~ were controlled trials.*
c. CORRECT: *Two studies were reported. Both of them were controlled trials.*
d. WRONG: *Two studies were ~~reported, both of them~~ were controlled trials.*

41. Tricky pair: **remainder/remaining**

Original sentence: *The remainder of this paper is organized as follows…*

Don't confuse *remainder* (noun) with *remaining* (adjective):

a. *In the remainder of this article, I will turn my attention to…*
b. *In the remaining sections, I will discuss…*

42. Key word: **in-depth**

Original sentence: *An in-depth analysis of _____ is not within the scope of this article.*

In-depth (deep or deeply) is very common in academic writing. It can be used in a number of ways:

a. *In this study we carried out an in-depth analysis of statistical data regarding the impact of the initiative.*
b. *The book provides an in-depth framework for understanding modern politics.*
c. *The role of flower therapy is explained in-depth at the end of this chapter.*

Now take the quiz on the next page to check your progress.

QUIZ 4

Correct the mistakes, if any, in sentences 1-6. Answers on page 66.

1. In the remaining of this section, I intend to describe the data in more detail.

2. Smith's research contradicts the two previous studies, both of them draw on large longitudinal datasets.

3. Section three discusses about policies of poverty reduction and their affect on wealth distribution.

4. The dataset comprises three separate tables, all of which are normalized to 3NF.

5. The questionnaire was comprised of 42 questions divided into three sections.

6. Section two provides key information in regard to the trial study.

CHAPTER 5
GENERAL LITERATURE REVIEW

This is the part of your paper where you refer extensively to relevant research and theory in the field. You should make connections between the studies you have read and where you position yourself among these studies. It is important to show your audience that you have actively engaged with the relevant body of knowledge your research is based on. Sentences 217-285 will help you do that.

A number of/Numerous scholars have...
217. conducted research on _____.
218. investigated why _____.
219. noted that _____.
220. correctly observed that _____.
221. examined the role of _____.
222. considered the implications of _____.
223. recognized the importance of _____.
224. sought to problematize _____.
225. pointed out that _____.
226. suggested that _____.
227. attempted to identify _____.
228. proposed theories to explain _____.
229. found evidence that _____.
230. sought to understand **phenomena**[43] such as _____.
231. offered explanations for _____.
232. argued that _____.
233. **contended**[44] that _____.
234. argued in favor of/against _____.
235. voiced concern about _____.
236. taken issue with _____.
237. grappled with the issue of _____.

238. openly questioned whether _____.
239. raised doubts regarding _____.
240. stressed the importance of _____.
241. carried out empirical studies on _____.
242. drawn parallels between _____ and _____.
243. turned their attention to _____.
244. provided empirical evidence supporting _____.
245. written extensively about _____.
246. made the claim that _____.
247. acknowledged the fact that _____.

248. It is generally agreed that _____.
249. Most of the research on _____ suggests _____.
250. Current research seems to indicate that _____.
251. Current studies appear to support the notion that _____.
252. Recent research has tended to show _____.
253. In the literature on _____, there seems to be general agreement that _____.
254. It is generally accepted wisdom that _____.
255. Empirical evidence appears to confirm the notion that _____.

On hedging:

An important feature of academic writing is the use of "hedging" (tentative language), which enables you to soften the tone of your assertions and make claims that are proportionate to the evidence available. In sentences 248-255, this is achieved through the use of adverbs (e.g.: generally), quantifiers (e.g.: most) and verbs such as suggest, tend, seem *and* appear. *Researchers in the humanities and social sciences often benefit from the judicious use of hedging. However, if you are writing a research paper in the natural sciences, you should use hedging more sparingly. If in doubt, ask your instructor first.*

256. Definitions of _____ emerging from _____ include _____.
257. The literature on _____ has its roots in _____.
258. Proponents of _____ have pointed out that _____.
259. Despite differences in _____, there are areas of agreement.

260. Another area of (dis)agreement among researchers is ____.
261. Most researchers working in the area of ____ **agree**[45] on/that ____.
262. Much of the debate over ____ has revolved around ____.
263. Much previous work on ____ has focused on ____.
264. A recent line of research has focused on ____.
265. ____ has generated an impressive amount of research.
266. Previous **research**[46] has supported the hypothesis that ____.
267. There is a growing body of research on ____.
268. Previous studies have demonstrated ____.
269. Laboratory-based studies have clearly shown ____.
270. A considerable **amount**[47] of research has focused on ____.
271. Past studies have yielded some important insights into ____.
272. Past studies have hinted at a link between ____ and ____.
273. A number of studies have explored the relationship between ____ and ____.
274. A recent line of research has established that ____.
275. The existing literature emphasizes ____.
276. The current literature on ____ suggests that ____.
277. The review of the literature shows that ____.
278. Current theories hypothesize that ____.
279. A widely accepted **hypothesis**[48] is that ____.
280. Empirical evidence has supported the claim that ____.
281. The idea that ____ is central to theories of ____.
282. While there is wide agreement that ____, views differ on ____.
283. While there is broad agreement that ____, it remains controversial whether ____.
284. While early studies suggested that ____, later research seems to indicate that ____.
285. While it is generally agreed that ____, there is less consensus over **whether or not**[49] ____.

GRAMMAR AND VOCABULARY TIPS 5

43. Singular vs. plural: **phenomenon/phenomena**

Original sentence: *A number of/Numerous scholars have sought to understand phenomena such as _____.*

Phenomena is the plural form of *phenomenon*. Use a plural verb after *phenomena*:

a. *These phenomena are not fully understood.*
b. *This phenomenon is not fully understood.*

44. Key word: **contention**

Original sentence: *A number of/Numerous scholars have contended that _____.*

Contention (opinion/disagreement), the noun derived from the verb *contend*, can be used as follows:

a. *This line of study remains a source of contention in the field of psychology.*
b. *It is our contention that this law is a gross infringement of our civil liberties.*
c. *In our view, there are three conclusive answers to these contentions.*

45. Tricky pair: **agree on/agree that**

Original sentence: *Most researchers working in the area of _____ agree on/that _____.*

You *agree on* something and *agree that* something is the case:

a. *The two studies agree on the most important points.*
b. *Nearly all studies agree that physical activity reduces the risk of diabetes.*

46. Count vs. non-count: **research/study**

Original sentence: *Previous research has supported the hypothesis that _____.*

Research is generally used as an uncountable noun; *study* is countable:

a. *My research shows that...* (NOT "My ~~researches~~ show that...")
b. *A new study shows that...* (NOT "~~A new research~~ shows that...")

47. Tricky pair: **amount/number**

Original sentence: *A considerable amount of research has focused on _____.*

Use *amount* with uncountable and abstract nouns (*amount of information, research, progress, money, love*) and *number* with countable nouns (*number of details, studies, people, times, respondents, participants*). Here's a tip to help you remember the difference:

Amount = How much...?
Number = How many...?

48. Spelling: **hypothesize/hypothesis**

Original sentence: *A widely accepted hypothesis is that _____.*

Don't confuse *hypothesize* with *hypothesis*:

a. *Hypothesize*: verb (American English)
b. *Hypothesise*: verb (British English)
c. *Hypothesis*: singular noun
d. *Hypotheses*: plural noun

49. Key phrase: **whether or not**

Original sentence: *While it is generally agreed that _____, there is less consensus over whether or not _____.*

Here are other common phrases with *whether or not*: *heated debate over whether or not..., uncertain as to whether or not..., conclusions about whether or not..., the issue of whether or not...*

Now take the quiz on the next page to check your progress.

QUIZ 5

Correct the mistakes, if any, in sentences 1-6. Answers on page 67.

1. There is still disagreement over if vitamin C can prevent colds.

2. A number of different hypothesis have been put forward.

3. A large amount of theories have been disproved.

4. Current research seem to suggest that this is an isolated phenomena.

5. The available evidences tend to refute those claims.

6. The next section considers the issue of whether or not voting should be mandatory.

CHAPTER 6
REFERENCING

When you submit an academic paper, you will be required to follow a style guide. A style guide determines, among other things, how in-text citations should appear:

a. Smith (1799, p.9) argues that…
b. Smith (1799) argues that… (p.9)
c. Smith argues that… (1799, p.9)

The three most frequently used style guides are APA (Publication Manual of the American Psychological Association), MLA (Modern Language Association's Style Manual) and CMOS (Chicago Manual of Style). Be sure to use the style guide recommended by your instructor, regardless of the way in which in-text citations are used in sentences 286-329.

286. Smith argues that _____.
287. Smith has argued that _____.
288. In his 1799 study, Smith argued that _____.
289. Smith supports the notion that _____.
290. Smith (1799) was the first to coin the term "_____."
291. Smith and Jones (1799, p.99) remind us that _____.
292. Smith and Jones, in their study of _____, found that _____.
293. Smith (1799) **poses**[50] the question, "_____?"
294. Proponents of _____ include Smith, who _____ (1799, p.99)
295. Those who maintain that _____ include Smith, who _____.
296. Smith's discussion of _____ openly acknowledges that _____.
297. The work of Smith et al. **demonstrates**[51] that _____.
298. Smith was one of the first to define _____ as _____.
299. Smith has advanced the hypothesis that _____.
300. Smith and Jones have put forward the hypothesis that _____.
301. Smith's impact on _____ has been widely examined.

302. **Each**[52] of these influential studies has claimed that ____.
303. The study carried out by Smith (1799) revealed that ____.
304. Smith's theoretical framework (1799, p.99) takes account of ____.
305. A number of studies ____. Specifically, Smith and Jones (1799, p.99) examined ____.
306. As an example of ____, consider the study of Smith (1979), which[53] ____.
307. Smith and Jones (1799) outlined several models for ____.
308. Smith (1799) provided one of the earliest discussions of ____.
309. Smith and Jones have carried out an extensive study on ____.
310. Smith et al. (1799) established a link between ____ and ____.
311. Several reports by Smith and Jones have found an **association**[54] between ____ and ____.
312. Smith argues that it is a misconception to view ____ as ____
313. In discussing ____, Smith argues that ____.
314. In his discussion of ____ (1799, p.99), Smith confirms the centrality of ____.
315. While Smith's findings indicate that ____, it has not yet been demonstrated that ____.
316. Although Smith argues that ____, a better way to **frame**[55] the issue is ____.
317. This finding is congruent with the work of Smith (1799), **which/who**[56] ____.
318. Smith (cited in Jones, 1799) defines ____ as ____.
319. As Smith (1799) points out from Jones' research, ____.
320. Smith's argument builds on Jones' in that ____.
321. Drawing on the work of Jones, Smith highlights ____.
322. Smith, **drawing on**[57] Jones, defined ____ as ____.
323. According to Smith, "____." Jones went even further and claimed that ____.
324. Smith claimed that ____. In a similar vein, Smith also found that ____.
325. Smith (cited in Jones, 1799) defines ____ as ____.

326. Smith claims that ____ (as cited in Jones, 1799, p. 99).
327. In this study, Smith et al. (1799) largely confirm Jones' findings.
328. In his 1799 study, Smith ____. Other scholars such as Jones have further analyzed ____.
329. Both Smith and Jones ____. However, while the **former** ____, the **latter**[58] ____.

GRAMMAR AND VOCABULARY TIPS 6

50. Key word: **pose**

Original sentence: *Smith (1799) poses the question, "____?"*

In this example, *pose* is a more formal way of saying *ask*. Another common meaning of *pose* is *represent*, and it is often used with the following words: *pose a (serious) problem, challenge, threat, risk.*

51. Subject/verb agreement: **complex subjects** (I)

Original sentence: *The work of Smith et al. demonstrates that ____.*

Notice that *demonstrates* agrees with *work* (*it*) rather than with *Smith et al.* (*they*).

52. Subject/verb agreement: **complex subjects** (II)

Original sentence: *Each of these influential studies has claimed that ____.*

Notice that the verb agrees with *each* rather than with the plural noun:

Each of the respondents was (NOT "~~were~~") *asked to complete a 10-item questionnaire.*

53. Relative clauses: **which/that**

Original sentence: *As an example of ____, consider the study of Smith (1979), which ____.*

When the relative pronoun *which* is preceded by a comma (i.e., when it adds extra information to a clause), it can't be replaced by *that*:

a. *These are the research questions which/that inspired the present study.*
b. *Smith's study, which* (NOT "~~that~~") *was published in 2015, has a number of flaws.*

54. Linking ideas: **association**

Original sentence: *Several reports by Smith and Jones have found an association between _____ and _____.*

You can also use *related* and *intertwined* to say that there is an *association* between two ideas:

a. *The problems of crime and unemployment are closely related.*
b. *Smith argued that domestic violence and substance abuse are inextricably intertwined.*

55. Key word: **frame**

Original sentence: *Although Smith argues that _____, a better way to frame the issue is _____.*

Here are other ways to use *frame* (formulate) as a verb: *frame public policies, your argument (in academic terms), your question (precisely), the debate (in terms of social issues), the issue (in a way that resonates with people).*

56. Relative clauses: **who/which**

Original sentence: *This finding is congruent with the work of Smith (1799), which/who _____.*

Use *which* to refer to Smith's work and *who* to refer to Smith himself. Remember you can't use *that* in either case. (See 53 on page 39.)

57. Key word: **draw**

Original sentence: *Smith, drawing on Jones, defined _____ as _____.*

In the last two examples, *draw on* means *base on*. Here are other common uses of *draw*:

a. *It is impossible to draw any firm conclusion from the results.* (reach)
b. *Smith drew an interesting analogy between music and language learning.* (establish)
c. *Jones' arguments have drawn a lot of criticism.* (attract)

58. Style: **former/latter**

Original sentence: *Both Smith and Jones _____. However, while the former _____, the latter _____.*

In formal writing, *former* refers to the first of two mentioned people or things, while *latter* refers to the second. They usually appear as a pair:

The questionnaires were distributed to teachers and students. The former were asked specific questions about methodology, while the latter answered more general questions.

Remember: *Former* is the first word. Both *former* and *first* start with "F." *Latter* is the last word. Both *latter* and *last* start with "L."

QUIZ 6

Correct the mistakes, if any, in sentences 1-6. Answers on page 67.

1. Houston's study, that dates back to the late 1980s, was extremely influential.

2. The questions were sent to all participants who answered them by e-mail.

3. Both issues are so intertwined as to be inseparable.

4. Ninety-five students were interviewed, and each of the interviews were digitally recorded.

5. Our findings suggest that students enjoy both grammar and pronunciation. They seem to believe that the former is as important as the latter.

6. Climate change poses a real threat to future generations.

CHAPTER 7
SAMPLING AND DATA COLLECTION

This is the part of your paper where you describe the process by which you attempted to answer the initial research question you posed. Sentences 330-444 will help you do that.

Participants (in this study) were...
330. members of _____.
331. selected from _____.
332. mostly of _____ origin/background.
333. selected based on _____.
334. assigned to a control group and a test group.
335. **randomly**[59] sampled from _____.
336. randomly selected based on _____.

The target population was...
337. composed of _____.
338. drawn from _____.
339. recruited from _____.
340. restricted to people (who) _____.
341. defined as _____.
342. categorized based on _____.

The sample for this study...
343. included _____.
344. consisted of _____.
345. comprised _____.
346. was taken from _____.
347. was randomly drawn from _____.
348. was limited to _____.

349. Each sampling unit consisted of _____.
350. A sample of [N] _____ was selected for **analysis**[60].
351. The subjects of this study consisted of _____.
352. A total of [N] subjects were divided based on _____.
353. Among the [N] eligible subjects, _____ participated in the study.
354. Among the eligible subjects, [N] refused to participate.
355. Eligible subjects were between the ages of _____ and _____.
356. [N] subjects were randomly assigned to _____.
357. The control (N=x) and experimental groups (N=y) were composed of _____.
358. The mean age was _____.
359. Among the study cohort, [N] participants met our eligibility criteria.
360. _____ was the sole **criterion**[61] for selection.

The present study employed a [qualitative/quantitative]...
361. approach that involved _____.
362. approach combining _____ and _____.
363. approach to investigate _____.
364. research design to investigate _____.
365. research methodology **exploring**[62] _____.
366. research method to examine _____.

367. The research design involved _____.
368. This study used a combination of qualitative and quantitative analysis tools.
369. The data collected were mostly qualitative/quantitative.
370. Data were collected through the use of _____.
371. The total number of respondents **was**[63] defined by _____.
372. A total of [N] responses were gathered from a sample of _____.
373. _____ was/were ascertained by means of _____.
374. Data were collected by means of _____.

375. The data for this study come from _____.
376. Additional data were gathered through _____.
377. **Data**[64] on _____ were not available.

For the purpose of this study…
378. _____ was measured with _____.
379. _____ is defined as follows: _____.
380. _____ was defined as _____.
381. _____ is defined as _____ if _____.
382. _____ was classified as _____.
383. _____ and _____ are not synonymous.
384. we used a dataset provided by _____.
385. [N] _____ were asked to _____.
386. we will adopt _____.

The survey was administered to [N] participants,…
387. **all of whom**[65] _____.
388. most of whom _____.
389. some of whom _____.
390. few of whom _____.
391. half of whom _____.
392. [N] of whom _____.
393. [N] % of whom _____.
394. of whom [N] % _____.

The survey included…
395. a variety of questions on _____.
396. a set of questions designed to _____.
397. a number of open-ended and multiple-choice questions.
398. questions to **determine**[66] _____.
399. an inventory of _____.
400. scales to measure _____.
401. questions taken from _____.
402. [N] questions, split evenly between _____ and _____.

403. We conducted in-depth interviews with _____.
404. The interview questions to elicit _____ were of [N] kinds: _____, _____ and _____.
405. The main purpose of the first type of questions was to _____.

All interviews…
406. ranged between _____ and _____ minutes/hours.
407. took place between _____ and _____.
408. were digitally recorded.
409. were audio/video taped.
410. were transcribed verbatim.
411. were coded and fully transcribed.

All interviews were conducted…
412. between _____ and _____.
413. in English (and _____).
414. within the premises of _____.
415. face-to-face.
416. by telephone/via Skype.

Participants completed a questionnaire…
417. to determine _____.
418. to elicit _____.
419. that measured _____.
420. that attempted to gain insight into _____.
421. designed to provide data on _____.
422. designed to evaluate/assess _____.
423. consisting of [N] **discrete**[67] items.

Participants completed a questionnaire in which they…
424. indicated (whether) _____.
425. were asked to _____.
426. provided information about _____.
427. rated _____ in terms of _____.
428. rated the importance of _____ on a [N]-point scale.

429. All participants were asked to read and sign a consent form.
430. From the [N] completed questionnaires, [N]% were fully usable.
431. The overall response rate was [N]%.
432. Self-reported data were gathered on gender, age and _____.
433. The association between _____ and _____ was examined using _____, with significance set at [N].
434. Next, _____ analyses were used to determine _____.
435. We examined whether _____. For this, we conducted two experiments in which _____.
436. I reviewed findings from a number of recent studies that _____.
437. _____ was based on participants' accounts of _____.
438. Fieldwork was undertaken over a **[N]-day**[68]/week/month/year period.

Full-text copies of _____ were accessed digitally/obtained from [source].
439. **potentially**[69] relevant studies
440. studies of possible relevance
441. potentially eligible articles
442. randomized trials
443. relevant legislation
444. relevant **theses**[70] and dissertations

GRAMMAR AND VOCABULARY TIPS 7

59. Key word: **random**

Original sentence: *Participants (in this study) were randomly sampled from* _____.

Both *random* (adjective) and *randomly* (adverb) are very common in academic writing. Study these examples:

a. *The names are listed in random order.*
b. *We interviewed a random sample of students.*
c. *Questionnaires were sent to a random selection of households.*
d. *The group to be studied was selected on a random basis.*
e. *The interviewees were chosen randomly.*
f. *Each doctor surveyed 15 patients selected randomly.*

60. Spelling: **analysis**

Original sentence: *A sample of [N]* _____ *was selected for analysis.*

a. *Analysis:* singular noun
b. *Analyses:* plural noun
c. *Analyze:* verb (American English)
d. *Analyse:* verb (British English)

61. Singular vs. plural: **criterion/criteria**

Original sentence: _____ *was the sole criterion for selection.*

Criteria is plural; *criterion* is singular:

a. *The criteria were* (NOT "was") *clear.*
b. *This was the main criterion* (NOT "criteria") *we used.*

62. Relative clauses: **reduced relative clauses** (I)

Original sentence: *The present study employed a [qualitative/quantitative] research methodology exploring _____.*

Notice how the *-ing* verb (*exploring*) is used to refer to the preceding word:

The present study employed a qualitative methodology exploring the subjects' attitudes to American culture.
= *The present study employed a qualitative methodology that explored the subjects' attitudes to American culture.*

63. Subject/verb agreement: **number**

Original sentence: *The total number of respondents was defined by _____.*

Notice that *was* agrees with *number* rather than *respondents*.

64. Subject/verb agreement: **data**

Original sentence: *Data on _____ were not available.*

You can use *data* as a mass noun (*the data is/the data shows*) or a count noun (*the data are/the data show*). Both are considered standard in modern English. Academic English, however, still tends to favor the use of a plural verb after *data*:

The data suggest that our initial hypotheses were correct.

65. Tricky pairs: **all** and **both**/**none** and **neither**

Original sentence: *The survey was administered to [N] participants, all of whom _____.*

Use *all, both, none* or *neither* before *whom* depending on the number of people being referred to:

a. *All of whom*: 3 people or more
b. *Both of whom*: 2 people
c. *None of whom*: 3 people or more
d. *Neither of whom*: 2 people

66. Key word: **determine**

Original sentence: The survey included questions to determine _____.

You can use a variety of structures after *determine*: *the number of…, the amount of…, the percentage of…, whether or not…, the extent of…, the extent to which…, the degree of…, the degree to which…*

67. Tricky pair: **discrete/discreet**

Original sentence: Participants completed a questionnaire consisting of [N] discrete items.

Don't confuse *discrete* (individual, separate) with *discreet* (quiet and cautious):

a. *For the purpose of this study, participants were divided into discrete categories.*
b. *My personal assistant is very discreet. I know my secrets are safe with him.*

68. Singular/plural: **compound adjectives**

Original sentence: Fieldwork was undertaken over a [N]-day/week/month/year period.

Notice the use a singular noun in phrases such as:

a. *A two-week experiment.* (NOT "a two-weeks experiment")
b. *A four-year project.* (NOT "a four-years project")

69. Spelling: **-ly adverbs**

Original sentence: Full-text copies of potentially relevant studies were accessed digitally/obtained from [source].

If you are not sure whether an adverb contains one or two "Ls", look at the adjective. If it already has an "L", there should be two:

a. *Potential/Potentially*
b. *Extreme/Extremely*
c. *Quick/Quickly*
d. *Real/Really*

70. Singular vs. plural: -**sis**/-**ses**

Original sentence: *Full-text copies of relevant theses and dissertations were accessed digitally/obtained from [source].*

Theses is the plural of *thesis*. Other words that follow this pattern include:

a. *analysis* (singular)/*analyses* (plural)
b. *hypothesis* (singular)/*hypotheses* (plural)
c. *diagnosis* (singular)/*diagnoses* (plural)

Now take the quiz on the next page to check your progress.

QUIZ 7

Correct the mistakes, if any, in sentences 1-6. Answers on page 68.

1. Twenty-five PhD thesis were analyzed.

2. In this study, we attempt to determine the extent to which these processes can be standardized.

3. The number of subjects affected by the disease were higher than expected.

4. The data were analyzed using the SAS statistical program.

5. Separate analysis were carried out, with each discreet item defined as a dependable variable.

6. Each criteria was awarded a value between 0 and 4.

CHAPTER 8
DATA ANALYSIS AND DISCUSSION

This section is in many ways the heart of your paper. It is where you tie together your initial research questions, the data you collected and the previous research that informed your thinking. In this section, you should also acknowledge the limitations of your study and, when appropriate, suggest future research avenues. Sentences 445-600 will help you do that.

445. This study used qualitative/quantitative techniques to analyze ____.
446. We analyzed the relationship between ____ and ____.
447. We conducted all analyses using ____.
448. The analysis was based on ____.
449. The data were analyzed using [N] different approaches.
450. Content analysis was **undertaken**[71] to determine ____.
451. The data were submitted to content analysis.
452. The data from ____ were **weighted**[72] to make them ____.

On the use of active/passive voice (4):
Sentences 445-447 are in the active voice, while 448-452 are in the passive voice. Different academic disciplines tend to favor one or the other, so be sure to follow the guidelines set by your institution.

453. The results analysis consists of [N] stages.
454. The datasets for ____ span the period from ____ to ____.
455. Before we analyze the data, it would be wise to ____.
456. Outside variables were excluded from ____.
457. Extraneous variables were controlled by ____.
458. ____ was considered a dependent/an independent variable.
459. Additional variables were derived from ____.

460. Data on several variables were used to _____.
461. The data were normalized by _____ to [N].
462. The correlation between _____ was calculated to evaluate _____.
463. Table [N] presents _____.
464. Table [N] and [N] highlight _____.
465. The percentages in the table represent _____.
466. Not included in table [N] is/are _____.
467. It can be **inferred**[73] from table [N] that _____.
468. A cursory glance at table [N] reveals that _____.
469. Figure [N] is a graphic summary of _____.
470. The horizontal axis describes _____, **while**[74] the vertical axis highlights _____.
471. The mean/median values of _____ are shown in figure/table [N].
472. Figure [N] shows the mean values for _____.
473. Table [N] shows the median values for _____.
474. There was a significant difference in mean values across _____.
475. There was a slight difference in median values across _____.
476. As shown in figure/table [N], a significant difference in mean/median levels was observed.
477. Table [N] shows the mean/median values (ranging from [N] to [N]) of _____.

Means and standard deviations...
478. were [N] and [N].
479. were determined through _____.
480. were obtained from _____.
481. were computed using _____.
482. were calculated for each _____.
483. are presented in table [N].
484. are reported in table [N].
485. for _____ are shown in table [N].

486. Results were considered significant if p</=/>[N].
487. There was no statistical difference between _____ and _____.

Statistical significance was...
488. accepted at the [N] level.
489. set at P = [N].
490. determined by _____.
491. assessed by _____.
492. reached in all cases.
493. not achieved due to _____.

494. A positive correlation was obtained between _____ and _____.
495. Correlations between _____ and _____ were negative and statistically significant.
496. Correlations between _____ and _____ were positive but statistically insignificant.
497. Significant correlations were obtained between _____ and _____.
498. No significant correlations were obtained between _____ and _____.
499. _____ was positively correlated with _____.
500. _____ correlated negatively with _____.

Our findings...
501. fall into [N] broad categories: _____.
502. can be divided into [N] categories: _____.
503. can be compared to results of earlier studies that _____.
504. provide strong evidence (that) _____.
505. reveal a high rate of _____.

The risk of bias...
506. was rated as low/high for each _____.
507. was low in _____, high in _____ and unclear in _____.
508. was evaluated according to _____.
509. in _____ was assessed by _____.

The results yielded…
510. some interesting findings.
511. no signs of _____.
512. no proof of _____.
513. no significant correlation between _____ and _____.
514. no statistically significant relationships between _____ and _____.
515. additional evidence of _____.

The data provide preliminary evidence…
516. and theoretical support for _____.
517. that _____ may be related to _____.
518. that _____ could be useful in _____.
519. for the theory described in section _____.
520. to suggest that _____.
521. of the extent to which _____.

The data provide convincing evidence…
522. in favor of _____.
523. against _____.
524. that _____.
525. showing that _____.
526. demonstrating that _____.
527. that _____ is a key component of _____.
528. of a link between _____ and _____.
529. of a strong association between _____ and _____.
530. against the hypothesis that _____.
531. for the claim that _____.

532. These figures suggest that _____ **regardless of**[75] _____.
533. These findings would suggest that _____.
534. _____ show(s) particularly interesting patterns.
535. [N] additional findings support these conclusions.
536. The present data are consistent with _____.
537. Our findings are consistent with previous results showing _____.

538. Results obtained by _____ are consistent with our findings.
539. As in previous studies, the results of this analysis confirm that _____.
540. An interesting side finding was that _____.
541. The general picture **emerging**[76] from the analysis is that _____.
542. Overall, these studies provide support for the validity of _____.
543. Taken altogether, the data presented here provide evidence that _____.
544. Contrary to our expectations, _____.
545. It might seem counterintuitive that _____, but _____.
546. These findings are less surprising if we consider _____.
547. A possible reason for this discrepancy might be that _____.
548. A possible interpretation of this finding is that _____.
549. A related idea which might explain _____ is _____.
550. There is still some doubt **as to**[77] whether _____.
551. The hypothesis that _____ needs further support.
552. A further complication for the present hypothesis is that _____.
553. Several findings of this study warrant further discussion, such as _____.
554. We would encourage researches to examine _____.
555. At present we are not in a position to determine _____.
556. In light of _____, few conclusions can be drawn from _____.
557. Given _____, our findings should not be over-interpreted.
558. Our findings suggest a need for greater _____.

Our findings are not generalizable…
559. beyond the study sample.
560. beyond the population studied.
561. beyond the participants interviewed.
562. beyond the subset examined.
563. beyond this study.
564. beyond this case study.
565. beyond this population.
566. to other settings.

567. to a larger population.
568. to the entire _____.
569. to _____ as a whole.
570. to every _____.
571. to all _____.

572. Our dataset _____ was limited to _____. **Therefore**[78], these findings are not generalizable beyond/to _____.

Future research will have to…
573. clarify (whether) _____.
574. confirm (whether) _____.
575. determine (whether) _____.
576. look into _____.
577. assess the extent to which _____.
578. shed light on _____.
579. address _____ in more detail.
580. ascertain the veracity of _____.
581. investigate to what extent _____.
582. meet the challenge of _____.

Future studies will have to…
583. explore _____.
584. continue to explore _____.
585. focus on _____.
586. concentrate on _____.
587. look at ways to _____.
588. consider how _____.
589. evaluate _____ against _____.
590. further investigate _____.
591. **further**[79] our understanding of _____.
592. investigate the role of _____.
593. isolate the effects of _____.
594. differentiate between _____ and _____.

595. address the issue of _____.
596. **take _____ into account.**[80]
597. account for _____.
598. examine the circumstances under which _____.
599. identify mechanisms through which _____.
600. clarify the relationship between _____ and _____.

GRAMMAR AND VOCABULARY TIPS 8

71. Key word: **undertake**

Original sentence: *Content analysis was undertaken to determine* _____.

The verb *undertake* (begin to do something) is frequently used in academic writing. You can *undertake an analysis, a task, a project, research, an investigation into something, an initiative to do something.*

72. Key word: **weight**

Original sentence: *The data from* _____ *were weighted to make them* _____.

The verb *weight* (NOT "~~weigh~~" in this case) is commonly used in academic writing. Study these examples:

a. *The sample was weighted to match the national average.*
b. *The results were weighted to allow for variations in the sample.*
c. *The data were weighted to represent the target population.*

73. Tricky pair: **infer/imply**

Original sentence: *It can be inferred from table [N] that* _____.

Infer and *imply* are opposites, like *go* and *come*, *take* and *bring*, *speak* and *hear*. *Imply* is to hint at something, while *infer* means to make an educated guess:

a. *From these facts we can infer that inflation has dropped.*
b. *The report implies that one million jobs might be lost.*

Remember: The speaker does the *implying*, while the listener does the *inferring*.

74. Linking ideas: **while/as opposed to/unlike**

Original sentence: *The horizontal axis describes _____, while the vertical axis highlights _____.*

While, as opposed to and *unlike* are used to express contrast:

a. *While the data might be limited in scope, the rate of success is significant.*
b. *Whereas previous research has focused on EFL, this study is mostly concerned with ESL.*
c. *Unlike recent studies on acupuncture, ours focuses on its mainstream appeal.*
d. *To eliminate outliers, we used median, as opposed to mean values.*

75. Style: alternatives to **regardless of**

Original sentence: *These figures suggest that _____ regardless of _____.*

Besides *regardless of*, you can also use *irrespective of* to say that X is not affected by Y. *Irrespective of* is slightly more formal. Remember: "Irregardless" is considered nonstandard.

76. Relative clauses: **reduced relative clauses with –ing** (II)

Original sentence: *The general picture emerging from the analysis is that _____.*

The use of the *-ing* form in *emerging* replaces a *that/which* relative clause. You can use reduced relative clauses with *-ing* to make your writing less wordy. Compare sentences A and B:

a. *The general picture emerging from the analysis is that...*
b. *The general picture that/which emerges from the analysis is that...*

77. Style: **as to**

Original sentence: *There is still some doubt as to whether _____.*

As to is a more formal way of saying *about*, and it is often followed by a *wh-* word:

a. *There is no consensus as to why this might be the case.*
b. *Decisions as to what constitutes risky behavior were made at the outset of the study.*
c. *Participants gave a number of suggestions as to how the issue could be addressed.*

78. Punctuation: **therefore**

Original sentence: *Our dataset _____ was limited to _____. Therefore, these findings are not generalizable beyond/to _____.*

Notice the use of periods, commas and semi-colons with *therefore* to express cause and consequence:

a. *Our findings may be biased. Therefore, further research is necessary.*
b. *Our findings may be biased; therefore, further research is necessary.*
c. *Our findings may be biased. Further research is, therefore, necessary.*

A comma can't precede *therefore* if it's followed by an independent clause:

"Our findings may be ~~biased, therefore, further~~ research is necessary."

79. Key word: **further**

Original sentence: *Future studies will have to further our understanding of _____.*

In examples a-c below, notice that the first *further* is an adverb that means *beyond what has already been done,* while the second one is a verb that means to *promote. Further* can also be used as an adjective, as shown in example c:

a. *The subject's health problems were further complicated by a previously-undetected heart condition.* (adverb)
b. *Subjects were asked how they intended to further their personal and professional development.* (verb)
c. *For further details, refer to page 22.* (adjective)

80. Key phrase: **take into account**

Original sentence: *Future studies will have to take _____ into account.*

When you take something into account (or take into account something), you consider it when judging a situation:

a. *We recommend that practitioners take recent research into account.*
b. *It is important to take into account the fact that participants might have misunderstood the question.*

Take [x] into account generally works better when [x] is a short word or phrase. *Take into account [x]* is preferable when [x] is a longer phrase.

Now take the quiz on the next page to check your progress.

QUIZ 8

Correct the mistakes, if any, in sentences 1-6. Answers on page 68.

1. These findings, therefore, provide evidence for a link between birth order and general intelligence.

2. The survey included questions as to whether respondents had experienced any health symptoms.

3. Further research should be undertaken to ascertain the veracity of these findings.

4. Table 1 shows the pre-test scores, as opposed to table 2 contains the post-test scores.

5. Each of these factors were weighted according to their relative importance.

6. To date, there has been little research on the consequences of e-cigarette use. Therefore, the present study seems especially relevant.

QUIZ ANSWERS

QUIZ 1

1. In the past few years, there HAS BEEN a great deal of controversy surrounding soy foods, mostly due to recent research.
2. The last four decades have seen incredible human progress across South America. CORRECT
3. Since the 1990s, there has been a dramatic increase in the number of people with Alzheimer's. CORRECT
4. Recent studies have RAISED a number of key questions regarding the impact of CCTV on crime.
5. In 2014, an important study by Smith et al. RAISED a number of concerns about online data collection.
6. It is not within the scope of this paper to propose solutions to this issue. This study is simply devoted to UNDERSTANDING the problem.

QUIZ 2

1. To the best of my knowledge, there IS relatively LITTLE RESEARCH/there ARE relatively FEW STUDIES in this area.
2. The evidence supporting a low-carb diet IS moderate at best.
3. The number of studies investigating the use of educational technology has dropped. CORRECT
4. In recent years, a number of scholars have addressed this issue. CORRECT
5. A number of longitudinal studies have examined this question; however, not all of them are replicable in other contexts. CORRECT
6. Despite claims to the contrary, there SEEMS to be ample evidence that this is the case.

QUIZ 3

1. The INFORMATION in chart 1 WAS collected in August 2015.
2. This study will try to determine WHETHER or not the initial hypotheses were valid.
3. At this point it is hard to ASSESS the extent to which these findings will have a sizeable impact on language teaching.
4. Although there SEEMS to be evidence that this is the case, the underlying mechanisms remain unclear.
5. This paper addresses the issue of urban violence and EXPLORES ways in which we can make our cities safer.
6. This study was undertaken as an attempt to assess the effects of meditation on blood pressure. CORRECT

QUIZ 4

1. In the REMAINDER of this section, I intend to describe the data in more detail.
2. Smith's research contradicts the two previous studies, both of WHICH draw on large longitudinal datasets.
3. Section three DISCUSSES policies of poverty reduction and their EFFECT on wealth distribution.
4. The dataset comprises three separate tables, all of which are normalized to 3NF. CORRECT
5. The questionnaire was comprised of 42 questions divided into three sections. CORRECT
6. Section two provides key information in regard to the trial study. CORRECT

QUIZ 5

1. There is still disagreement over WHETHER vitamin C can prevent colds.
2. A number of different HYPOTHESES have been put forward.
3. A large NUMBER of theories have been disproved.
4. Current research SEEMS to suggest that this is an isolated PHENOMENON.
5. The available EVIDENCE TENDS to refute those claims.
6. The next section considers the issue of whether or not voting should be mandatory. CORRECT

QUIZ 6

1. Houston's study, WHICH dates back to the late 1980s, was extremely influential.
2. The questions were sent to all PARTICIPANTS, WHO answered them by e-mail.
3. Both issues are so intertwined as to be inseparable. CORRECT
4. Ninety-five students were interviewed, and each of the interviews WAS digitally recorded.
5. Our findings suggest that students enjoy both grammar and pronunciation. They seem to believe that the former is as important as the latter. CORRECT
6. Climate change poses a real threat to future generations. CORRECT

QUIZ 7

1. Twenty-five PhD THESES were analyzed.
2. In this study, we attempt to determine the extent to which these processes can be standardized. CORRECT
3. The number of subjects affected by the disease WAS higher than expected.
4. The data were analyzed using the SAS statistical program. CORRECT
5. Separate ANALYSES were carried out, with each DISCRETE item defined as a dependable variable.
6. Each CRITERION was awarded a value between 0 and 4.

QUIZ 8

1. These findings, therefore, provide evidence for a link between birth order and general intelligence. CORRECT
2. The survey included questions as to whether respondents had experienced any health symptoms. CORRECT
3. Further research should be undertaken to ascertain the veracity of these findings. CORRECT
4. Table 1 shows the pre-test scores, WHILE table 2 contains the post-test scores.
5. Each of these factors WAS weighted according to their relative importance.
6. To date, there has been little research on the consequences of e-cigarette use. Therefore, the present study seems especially relevant. CORRECT

HOW THIS BOOK CAME INTO BEING

I first felt the need for a book like this back in 1998, when I did my MA in Applied Linguistics at Lancaster University (UK).

Whenever I started a new assignment, I usually knew exactly what I wanted to say and had no trouble organizing my ideas. What I lacked was a wider repertoire of sentences like "A cursory glance at […] reveals that […]" or "[…] is beyond the scope of this paper." Without that kind of language, I feared I would never truly belong to that kind of discourse community.

So here's what I used to do: After each and every scientific article I read, I made a list of useful phrases and sentence "templates" that I could include in my own writing. This turned out to be a wise move. When I eventually wrote my dissertation, I was able to use at least 25-30% of the hundreds of sentences I'd compiled.

Fortunately, I never deleted that list.

Back in 2013, as I was purging some old files, I stumbled upon the original Word document and wondered if other people might find my list useful. So I handpicked 70 sentences and turned them into a blog post, which, at the time, I hastily dismissed as a novelty no one would pay attention to.

I couldn't have been more wrong.

To my surprise, those 70 sentences went on to become my most popular post to date, with an average of 700 daily visits. It definitely looked as if I was on to something.

So, one day, I had a crazy idea: What if that blog post became a book?

So, in January 2015, I started compiling a brand new list, which forced me to read hundreds - and I mean literally hundreds- of academic papers beyond the field of Applied Linguistics (my area of expertise). I read lab reports, medical experiments, doctoral theses on urban planning, literature reviews on quantum physics, you name it. By December, I had amassed nearly a thousand sentence frames. But the book was still far from finished, of course.

The next step was to organize those sentences logically, check them for naturalness/frequency against corpus data, trim the list down to 600 items and write language tips that both native and non-native speakers might find useful.

And that was the part that nearly drove me insane. I lost count of the number of times I considered scrapping the whole project, but a little voice inside my head urged me to keep going.

And I'm glad I did.

As of October 2020, *The Only Academic Phrasebook You'll Ever Need* has sold over 25,000 copies and helped thousands of academic writers in at least nine different countries.

Thanks, again, for buying this book. Here's how you can reach me:

luizotaviobarros@gmail.com
luizotavio.com

Luiz Otávio Barros
October 2020

Printed in Great Britain
by Amazon

43334879R00047